AMSTERDAM TRAVEL GUIDE 2023

A Comprehensive Guide to the City of Canals

Earline L. Jones

This book is a work of non-fiction. The views expressed are solely those of the author and do not necessarily reflect the views of the publisher, and the publisher hereby disclaims any responsibility for them.

TABLE OF CONTENTS

Authors Note

As you hold this Amsterdam travel guide in your hands, you are about to embark on a journey through one of the most beautiful and vibrant cities in the world. From the winding canals that lace through the city, to the colorful tulips that bloom in spring, Amsterdam is a place that will captivate your senses and capture your heart. The rich history and culture of this city is evident in every corner, from the 17th century houses lining the canals, to the world-renowned museums that showcase the works of some of the greatest artists of all time.

But Amsterdam is not just about its picturesque beauty and historical significance. It is also a city that pulsates with energy, where locals and tourists alike gather to enjoy the delicious food, lively nightlife and endless entertainment options. Whether you're walking along the bustling streets or relaxing in one of the many parks, Amsterdam has a way of making you feel alive.

As you explore this city, you will find that Amsterdam has something for everyone. For the art lovers, there are museums such as the Van Gogh Museum and the Rijksmuseum, which house some of the most impressive collections in the world. For the history buffs, there are landmarks such as the Anne Frank House, which offers a sobering look at the city's past. For the foodies, there are countless cafes, restaurants and street vendors serving up traditional Dutch cuisine. And for those looking for a little fun, Amsterdam's famous Red Light District and Coffeeshops offer a unique and exciting experience.

As you flip through the pages of this guide, you will be guided through the must-see attractions and hidden gems that make Amsterdam so special. But don't let this guide limit your experience. Allow yourself to wander and discover the city on your own terms. Let Amsterdam surprise you with its unexpected delights and leave a lasting impression on your soul. From the charming streets of the Jordaan neighborhood, to the tranquil beauty of the Vondelpark, Amsterdam will leave you enchanted. This guide is simply a starting point, but the memories you create here will last a lifetime. So pack your bags, grab your camera and get ready to fall in love with Amsterdam.

CHAPTER 1: Introduction to Amsterdam - A Brief History And Overview Of The City

Discovering Amsterdam's History

Amsterdam, the capital of the Netherlands, has a rich and diverse history that spans centuries. The city was originally a small fishing village, founded in the 12th century on the banks of the Amstel River. The name Amsterdam comes from the combination of the words 'Amstel' and 'dam', referring to the dam built in the river to protect the village from flooding.

As the village grew, it became an important trading center and port, thanks to its strategic location at the intersection of several trade routes. In the 14th century, Amsterdam became a city and received its city rights. During the 15th and 16th century, the city experienced a period of prosperity and growth, as it became a center of trade, especially in textiles.

The Dutch Golden Age, which began in the 17th century, was a period of great prosperity and cultural achievements for Amsterdam. The city became one of the most important trading centers in the world, with a particular focus on trade with Asia, the Americas, and Africa. This prosperity led to a significant expansion of the city, and the construction of the famous canals, which were built to improve transportation and defend the city.

During this time, Amsterdam was also a leader in the arts and sciences. The city was home to many famous artists, such as Rembrandt, Vermeer and Frans Hals, and thinkers, such as Descartes and Spinoza. Many of these artists and thinkers were immigrants from other parts of Europe, and this influx of immigrants led to a diverse and multicultural society.

However, the 18th century saw the decline of Amsterdam's prosperity and the decline of the Dutch Republic. The city's economy shifted from trade to industry, but it never regained its former glory. In the 19th century, Amsterdam underwent a period of modernization, with the construction of new buildings and infrastructure, and the city continued to grow and expand.

The 20th century was marked by World War II, during which Amsterdam was occupied by the Nazis. The city suffered heavy damage during the war, and many of its historic buildings were destroyed. After the war, the city underwent a period of reconstruction and modernization. Amsterdam has since become a popular tourist destination, known for its beautiful architecture, museums, and canals. Today, Amsterdam is a vibrant and cosmopolitan city that combines its rich history with a modern and progressive culture.

Understanding The City's Culture

Amsterdam is renowned for its liberal and open-minded culture. The city is famous for its coffee shops, where cannabis can be purchased and consumed legally, and its red-light district, which is a major tourist attraction. However, Amsterdam is also home to many museums, art galleries, and cultural institutions, showcasing the city's rich history, art, and culture.

The city's museums and art galleries are world-renowned and include the Van Gogh Museum, which houses the largest collection of Van Gogh's paintings in the world, the Rijksmuseum, which is dedicated to Dutch art and history, and the Stedelijk Museum, which focuses on contemporary art.

Amsterdam is also known for its vibrant nightlife, with a wide range of bars, clubs, and music venues. The city also hosts numerous festivals and events throughout the year, including the famous Amsterdam Dance Event, which is one of the world's largest electronic music festivals, and the Holland Festival, which is a month-long festival of performing arts.

The city also has a strong tradition of cycling, with over 800,000 bicycles in the city and more bicycles than inhabitants. The cycling culture is so ingrained in the city that it is considered one of the most bike-friendly cities in the world.

Amsterdam is also a melting pot of cultures, and the city's diverse population is reflected in its vibrant and varied food scene, which offers a wide range of international cuisines. From traditional Dutch dishes such as stroopwafels, bitterballen, and stroganoff to international cuisine like Indonesian and Surinamese food. You can find a little bit of everything in Amsterdam.

Finally, Amsterdam is a very tolerant and open-minded city, and visitors will find a wide range of cultural and LGBTQ+ friendly events and festivals throughout the year. The city has a strong focus on sustainability, with many green initiatives and a strong commitment to protecting the environment.

Tips For Navigating The City

Get around by bike or foot: Amsterdam is a relatively small city and the best way to explore it is by foot or by bike. Not only is it a great way to see the city, but it also helps to avoid the crowds and traffic. Bicycling is a way of life in Amsterdam, and the city has an extensive network of bike lanes and paths. If you decide to rent a bike, be sure to lock it up properly when you're not using it as bike theft is a common issue in the city.

Avoid peak tourist season: Amsterdam is a popular destination, and during peak tourist season (May-September) the city can get very crowded. To avoid the crowds, consider visiting the city during the shoulder seasons (April, October) when the weather is still pleasant and the crowds are thinner.

Take a canal cruise: Amsterdam's canals are one of the city's defining features, and a canal cruise is an excellent way to see the city from a different perspective. Many companies offer canal cruises, and it's a great way to learn about the history of the city and see some of Amsterdam's most famous landmarks.

Explore the lesser-known neighborhoods: While Amsterdam's city center is full of sights and attractions, it can also be quite touristy. To experience the city like a local, consider visiting some of Amsterdam's lesser-known neighborhoods such as Jordaan, De Pijp, or Oost. These areas offer a glimpse into Amsterdam's authentic culture and character, and they are home to many independent shops, cafes, and restaurants.

Be aware of your surroundings: Amsterdam is a safe city, but it's still important to take precautions and be aware of your surroundings. Be mindful of pickpockets and keep your valuables close. Also, be aware of the city's open drug policy, as smoking marijuana is legal in Amsterdam but smoking anything in public is prohibited.

Use public transportation: Amsterdam's public transportation system is reliable and efficient. Trams, buses, and metro are all well-connected and can take you to most parts of the city. The city also has an extensive network of ferries, which are a great way to get around if you're staying on the outskirts of the city.

Plan ahead: Amsterdam is a popular destination, so it's wise to plan ahead to avoid disappointment. Many of the city's top attractions require advance reservations, so be sure to book your tickets in advance to ensure you get to see everything you want to see.

Keep an open mind: Amsterdam is a city that celebrates diversity, and it's important to keep an open mind when exploring the city. Whether it's the city's liberal drug policy, the red-light district or the city's diverse population, Amsterdam is a city that challenges conventions and stereotypes.

CHAPTER 2: The Canals Of Amsterdam - A Boat Tour Of The Iconic Waterways

Exploring The Canals By Boat

Amsterdam is a city known for its iconic canals, and one of the best ways to experience them is by boat. Taking a boat tour of the canals is a must-do for any visitor to the city, as it offers a unique perspective on the city and its history.

The boat tour starts at the central station, where you will board a traditional Dutch boat, known as a "sloep". The boat is small and intimate, with seating for up to 12 passengers. The tour guide will provide a commentary on the history of the canals, pointing out the many beautiful buildings and landmarks along the way.

As you make your way through the canals, you will pass under low bridges and through narrow canals. The guide will tell you about the history of the canals and how they were built to connect the city to the sea. You will also learn about the different types of boats that are used on the canals, including the iconic Dutch houseboats.

One of the highlights of the tour is passing through the UNESCO World Heritage-listed Canal Ring. This is a group of 17th-century canals that were built to connect the city to the sea. The canals are lined with beautiful houses and buildings, many of which date back to the 17th century. The tour guide will point out the most notable buildings, including the Anne Frank House, the Westerkerk and the Magere Brug.

The tour also takes you through the Jordaan, one of Amsterdam's most picturesque neighbourhoods. This is an area that is known for its narrow streets, canals, and beautiful houses. The tour guide will point out some of the famous residents of the Jordaan, including the famous Dutch artist, Rembrandt.

Canalside Cafes And Restaurants

One of the best things about taking a boat tour of the canals is that you can stop at canalside cafes and restaurants along the way. Amsterdam is known for its vibrant café culture, and the canalside cafes are the perfect place to experience it. The tour guide will take you to some of the most popular cafes and restaurants along the way, where you can stop for a drink or a bite to eat. Some of the most popular cafes and restaurants include the Café de Jaren, which is located on the Nieuwe Doelenstraat, and the De Pijp, which is located on the Albert Cuypstraat.

The Café de Jaren is a popular spot for tourists and locals alike. It is located on the Nieuwe Doelenstraat, which is one of the most picturesque streets in Amsterdam. The café offers a wide selection of beers, wines, and cocktails, as well as a menu of traditional Dutch dishes. You can enjoy a delicious meal while taking in the beautiful view of the canals. The café also has an outdoor terrace, where you can sit and enjoy your meal in the sunshine.

The De Pijp is another popular canalside café. It is located on the Albert Cuypstraat, which is known for its vibrant street market. The café offers a selection of beers, wines, and cocktails, as well as a menu of traditional Dutch dishes. The café has an outdoor terrace, where you can sit and watch the world go by. The café is also popular with locals and tourists alike, and is a great place to meet new people and make friends.

Canalside dining is a unique and enjoyable experience that you shouldn't miss when you visit Amsterdam. It's a perfect blend of traditional Dutch cuisine, beautiful views, and a lively atmosphere. The canalside cafes and restaurants are a must-visit for anyone looking to experience the city's vibrant café culture and take in the beautiful views of the canals.

Unique Canal-side Activities

One of the best things about exploring the canals of Amsterdam is that there are so many unique and exciting activities to experience. From renting a boat and cycling along the canals to swimming in the waterways and visiting canalside markets, there's something for everyone to enjoy.

Renting a boat: If you want to experience the canals on your own terms, renting a boat is a must-do. You can choose from different types of boats, such as traditional Dutch boats, electric boats, or even pedal boats. You can explore the canals at your own pace, taking in the sights and sounds of the city, and even discover hidden gems along the way.

Canalside cycling: Amsterdam is known for its cycling culture, and the canalside paths are the perfect place to explore on two wheels. You can rent a bike and cycle along the canals, taking in the beautiful architecture, the houseboats, and the bustling street life. You will also find many bike rental shops around the city center.

Canalside markets: Amsterdam is home to many canalside markets, where you can find a wide variety of local products, including fresh produce, cheese, and crafts. The Albert Cuyp market is a popular spot, and is open every day except

Sunday. You can also find many street vendors along the canals, selling everything from flowers to souvenirs.

Canalside art: Amsterdam is home to many canalside art galleries and shops, where you can find a wide variety of local art and crafts. The Jordaan neighbourhood is particularly known for its art galleries, and is a great place to explore if you're interested in Dutch art. You can also find street art along the canals, showcasing the work of local artists.

Canalside swimming: If you're looking for something a bit different, you can even take a dip in the canals. There are a few places in Amsterdam where you can swim in the canals, including the Oosterdok, which is a popular spot for swimmers.

From exploring the canals by boat, visiting canalside cafes and restaurants, to trying out unique canal-side activities, Amsterdam's iconic waterways offer a truly unique and exciting experience that you'll never forget.

CHAPTER 3: The Rijksmuseum - A Visit To The Dutch National Museum

Exploring The Rijksmuseum's Art Collection

The Rijksmuseum's art collection is one of the most extensive and diverse in the world, spanning over 800 years of Dutch history and culture. The collection is divided into several different sections, each dedicated to a specific period or theme.

One of the most important sections of the collection is the Dutch Golden Age Paintings, which is considered one of the most important collections of 17th-century art in the world. The collection includes masterpieces by famous Dutch artists such as Rembrandt, Vermeer, and Hals, as well as lesser-known but equally talented artists. Some of the most iconic pieces in this section include Rembrandt's "The Night

Watch," Vermeer's "Girl with a Pearl Earring," and Hals' "The Laughing Cavalier."

Another important section of the collection is the Asian art section, which is one of the most underrated but most impressive collections in the world. The collection includes works from China, Japan, and Indonesia, and it is a must-see for anyone interested in Asian art and culture. The section includes a range of different mediums, including ceramics, lacquerware, and textiles.

The Rijksmuseum's collection also includes a significant number of sculptures, decorative arts, and applied arts. The collection includes works by famous Dutch sculptors such as Hendrick de Keyser and Rombout Verhulst, as well as beautiful examples of Delftware, silverware, and furniture. These works provide a unique insight into the everyday life and culture of the Netherlands during different periods.

The collection also includes a section dedicated to prints and drawings, which is a great way to discover new and exciting artists and learn more about the history of art. The section includes works by famous Dutch artists such as Rembrandt, Van Gogh, and Degas, as well as works by lesser-known artists.

Discovering The Hidden Gems Within The Museum

The Rijksmuseum is a treasure trove of art and artifacts, and while the collection of Dutch Golden Age paintings is undoubtedly the main attraction, there are many hidden gems within the museum that are often overlooked by visitors. The museum's collection of Asian art is one of the most underrated and yet most impressive collections in the world. The collection includes works from China, Japan, and Indonesia, and it is a must-see for anyone interested in Asian art and culture.

The Asian art collection at the Rijksmuseum is vast and diverse, spanning over 2,000 years of history. Visitors can explore the collection of Chinese ceramics, which includes some of the most beautiful and intricate pieces of pottery in the world. The collection also includes a range of Chinese jade carvings, which are considered some of the most valuable works of art in the world.

The collection of Japanese art at the Rijksmuseum is also impressive and includes a range of works from different periods of Japanese history. Visitors can explore the collection of ukiyo-e woodblock prints, which are considered some of the most iconic works of Japanese art. The collection also includes a range of Japanese lacquerware, which is known for its intricate and delicate designs.

The collection of Indonesian art at the Rijksmuseum is also worth exploring. The collection includes a range of works from different periods of Indonesian history, including traditional textiles, sculptures, and batik. The collection is a great way to discover the rich culture and history of Indonesia.

Another hidden gem within the museum is the collection of prints and drawings. The collection includes works by famous Dutch artists such as Rembrandt, Van Gogh, and

Degas, as well as works by lesser-known artists. The collection is a great way to discover new and exciting artists and learn more about the history of art. The museum's collection of prints and drawings are often overlooked by visitors, but it is a must-see for anyone interested in the history of art.

Virtual Tours and Special Exhibitions

The Rijksmuseum offers a range of virtual tours and special exhibitions that allow visitors to explore the museum's collection from the comfort of their own home. The virtual tours are interactive and allow visitors to explore the museum's collection in a way that is not possible in person.

The virtual tours are available on the museum's website and can be accessed from any device with internet access. Visitors can explore the museum's collection of Dutch Golden Age paintings, sculptures, decorative arts, and applied arts. The virtual tours also include audio and video guides that provide additional information and context about the works of art on display.

In addition to the virtual tours, the museum also hosts a range of special exhibitions throughout the year. These exhibitions are a great way to discover new and exciting works of art and learn more about the history of art. The special exhibitions focus on specific themes or artists, and they often include works of art that are not on permanent display in the museum.

The museum's website also provides information about upcoming special exhibitions and virtual tours, so visitors can plan their virtual visit in advance. The museum also offers live streaming events and online lectures, which provide visitors with an opportunity to learn more about the art and artifacts on display.

In conclusion, The Rijksmuseum's virtual tours and special exhibitions are a great way to explore the museum's collection and discover new and exciting works of art from the comfort of your own home. The interactive tours and special exhibitions provide visitors with an opportunity to learn more about the art and artifacts on display and gain a deeper understanding of the history of art. So, whether you are unable to visit the museum in person or just want to explore the collection from the comfort of your own home, make sure to check out the Rijksmuseum's virtual tours and special exhibitions.

The Rijksmuseum

CHAPTER 4: The Anne Frank House - A Walk Through History

Visiting The Anne Frank House

The Anne Frank House is a must-see destination for anyone visiting Amsterdam. It is a powerful and poignant reminder of the atrocities that occurred during World War II and a testament to the resilience and courage of the human spirit. The house is open to the public and is located on Prinsengracht 263 in Amsterdam.

Upon arriving at the Anne Frank House, visitors are greeted by the museum's bookstore and gift shop. The bookstore offers a wide selection of books, including the original diary of Anne Frank, as well as souvenirs and gifts. After purchasing your tickets, visitors will then proceed to the museum's entrance.

The museum's entrance is a replica of the bookcase that concealed the entrance to the secret annex. As you step inside, you are immediately transported back in time to a world of fear and uncertainty. Visitors are given an audio guide that provides a detailed history of the Frank family, the secret annex, and the events that occurred during World War II.

The museum is divided into two parts: the Secret Annex and the museum's permanent exhibition. The Secret Annex is where the Frank family and their fellow residents lived in hiding for two years. Visitors can walk through the cramped and cramped living quarters and see where the family slept, ate, and spent their time. The museum's permanent exhibition provides a detailed history of the Holocaust and the events that led to the Frank family's hiding.

Visiting the Anne Frank House is an emotional experience, and it is not uncommon for visitors to be moved to tears. The museum is a powerful and poignant reminder of the atrocities that occurred during World War II and a testament to the resilience and courage of the human spirit. It is a must-see destination for anyone visiting Amsterdam and is open to visitors every day, except on Yom Kippur and Christmas day.

Discovering The Secret Annex

The secret annex is where the Frank family and their fellow residents lived in hiding for two years. The space was cramped and cramped, with no natural light, and it is hard not to feel a sense of claustrophobia as you walk through the rooms.

The first room visitors enter is the living room, which was shared by all the residents. The room is small and sparsely furnished, with a couch and a few chairs. The walls are adorned with pictures of movie stars, which were a source of comfort and distraction for the residents. The atmosphere in the living room is somber, and it is hard not to imagine the fear and uncertainty that the residents must have felt as they lived in hiding.

The next room is the kitchen, which was also shared by all the residents. The kitchen was the heart of the secret annex, and it was here that the residents would cook, eat, and spend time together. The space is small and cramped, with a small stove, a sink, and a table. Visitors can see the original pots and pans that were used by the residents, as well as a replica of the food that they would have eaten.

The bedrooms are also located on the first floor. The rooms are small and cramped, with bunk beds and minimal furnishings. Visitors can see the beds where Anne and her sister Margot slept, and the room where the Frank family's helpers, Miep Gies and Bep Voskuijl, slept. The bedrooms are a powerful reminder of the sacrifices that the residents of the secret annex had to make in order to survive.

The second floor of the secret annex is where Anne wrote her diary. The room is small and cramped, with a desk, a chair, and a window. Visitors can see the original diary, which is on display in a glass case. The diary is a powerful reminder of the resilience and courage of Anne Frank, and it is a powerful reminder of the impact that one person's words can have on the world.

Overall, the secret annex is a powerful and poignant reminder of the atrocities that occurred during World War II, and a testament to the resilience and courage of the human spirit. It is a powerful reminder of the importance of tolerance and acceptance, and it is a powerful tool for teaching about the Holocaust.

Learning About The Impact Of Anne's Diary

The Anne Frank House is not just a powerful reminder of the atrocities that occurred during World War II, it is also a testament to the power of the written word. Anne Frank's diary, which she wrote while in hiding in the secret annex, is one of the most widely read books in the world. It is a powerful reminder of the impact that one person's words can have on the world.

The diary was written by Anne between June 12, 1942, and August 1, 1944. She wrote it in a small notebook, which she had received as a birthday present. She wrote about her daily life in the secret annex, her thoughts and feelings, and her hopes for the future. She wrote about the fear and uncertainty that she and her family faced, and about the isolation and loneliness that they experienced.

The diary was discovered by Miep Gies, one of the Frank family's helpers, after the family was arrested. Gies saved the diary, and after the war, she gave it to Anne's father, Otto Frank. He published the diary in 1947, and it has since been translated into more than 60 languages.

The diary has had a profound impact on the world. It has been read by millions of people, and it has been the subject of countless books, articles, and documentaries. It has been used as a tool for teaching about the Holocaust, and it has been used to promote tolerance and acceptance. The diary has also been used as a tool for educating people about the importance of learning about the past in order to understand the present and the future.

The diary is a powerful reminder of the importance of education, and it is a powerful reminder of the importance of learning about the past in order to understand the present and the future. It is also a powerful reminder of the importance of tolerance and acceptance, and it is a powerful reminder of the importance of speaking out against injustice and oppression.

The diary is a powerful tool for teaching about the Holocaust, and it is a powerful reminder of the importance of learning about the past in order to understand the present and the future. It is also a powerful reminder of the importance of tolerance and acceptance, and it is a powerful reminder of the importance of speaking out against injustice and oppression.

The Anne Frank House

CHAPTER 5: The Heineken Experience - A Tour Of The Famous Brewery

Tasting The Beer At The Heineken Brewery

The tour of the Heineken brewery starts with a taste of the product, and it's a great way to whet your appetite for the rest of the experience. The brewery is located in the heart of Amsterdam, in a historic building that was first built in 1867. Visitors are taken through the brewing process, from the raw ingredients to the finished product, and get to see the huge copper kettles where the beer is cursed.

Visitors will learn about the various steps involved in brewing the beer, including mashing, boiling, fermenting, and aging. They will also get to see the different types of equipment used in the brewing process, such as the malt mill, the lauter tun, and the brew kettle. The tour guide will provide detailed explanations of the brewing process, making it easy for visitors to understand even if they have no prior knowledge of brewing.

After the tour, visitors are taken to the tasting room where they get to sample the famous Heineken lager. The beer is served in a special glass that has been designed to enhance the flavor and aroma of the beer. The tour guide will provide information about the different flavors and aromas of the beer, and will also give tips on how to best enjoy the beer.

The tasting experience is a great way to end the tour, as it allows visitors to savor the taste of the beer in a relaxed and enjoyable setting. It's a great opportunity to try the beer and compare it to other beers you may have tried before. Visitors can also purchase a bottle or a can of Heineken beer to take home as a souvenir.

Overall, the tasting experience at the Heineken brewery is a great way to learn about the brewing process and to enjoy the taste of the famous lager. It's a great addition to the tour and provides visitors with a complete and immersive experience. So, it's a must-visit destination for any beer lover.

Learning The History Of Heineken Beer

The Heineken Experience offers visitors a chance to learn about the rich history of the brewery and the Heineken family. The tour starts with an introduction to the Heineken family and their involvement in the beer industry, which dates back to 1873 when Gerard Heineken purchased a small brewery in Amsterdam. Visitors learn about how the brewery has grown and evolved over the years, and how it has become one of the most recognizable brands in the world.

The tour also covers the history of the brewing process, and how Heineken has been able to maintain its traditional brewing methods while still adapting to modern techniques. Visitors learn about the different ingredients that are used to make the beer, including the unique A-yeast that has been used in the brewing process since the 1800s.

One of the most interesting aspects of the tour is the visit to the Heineken family's private collection. Visitors are able to see some of the company's most iconic artifacts, such as old bottles, cans, and advertising materials. This is a great opportunity to see how the brewery and the brand have evolved over the years and to learn about some of the key moments in the company's history.

Enjoying The Interactive Exhibits

The Heineken Experience offers a variety of interactive exhibits that are designed to make the tour more fun and engaging. One of the highlights is the "Brew U" experience, where visitors can learn about the brewing process and even have a go at brewing their own beer. This interactive exhibit is a great opportunity for visitors to get hands-on experience of the brewing process and to take home their own unique beer.

Another popular exhibit is the virtual reality experience, which takes visitors through the brewing process and gives them a glimpse into the world of brewing. The VR experience allows visitors to explore the brewery and learn about the different ingredients and equipment used in the brewing process.

In addition to the virtual reality experience, there is also a game that allows visitors to test their knowledge of the brewery and the beer. The game is a fun and interactive way to learn about the brewery and the beer, and it's a great way to engage with other visitors.

The Heineken Experience is a great way to learn about the history of the brewery and the beer, and to enjoy a taste of the famous lager. It's a great destination for beer lovers, and it's a great way to experience Amsterdam's rich history and culture. So if you're planning a trip to Amsterdam, make sure you add the Heineken Experience to your itinerary.

CHAPTER 6: The Van Gogh Museum - A Look At The Art And Life Of Vincent Van Gogh

Exploring The Paintings And Drawings Of Van Gogh

The Van Gogh Museum is home to over 200 paintings and 500 drawings by the artist, making it one of the most comprehensive collections of his work in the world. Visitors can take a chronological journey through the artist's life, starting with his early drawings and moving on to his later masterpieces.

One of the highlights of the museum is the opportunity to see some of Van Gogh's most famous works up close, including "The Potato Eaters," "Sunflowers," and "Irises." These paintings are known for their bold use of color and expressive brushstrokes, which showcase the artist's unique style and vision. "The Potato Eaters" was Van Gogh's first real masterpiece and was painted in 1885. The painting is considered as a masterpiece as it is an early representation of the artist's use of bold colors and thick brushstrokes. The painting depicts a poor peasant family eating potatoes, and it's considered a symbol of the artist's connection to the working-class.

"Sunflowers" is one of Van Gogh's most famous works and is considered a masterpiece. This series of paintings was created during the artist's stay in Arles, France, in 1888 and 1889. The paintings depict sunflowers in a vase and are known for their bold use of color and thick brushstrokes. The series is considered a masterpiece as it is an early representation of the artist's use of bold colors and thick brushstrokes.

"Irises" is another masterpiece of the artist, and it was painted in 1889 during the artist's stay in the Saint-Paul-de-Mausole asylum in Saint-Rémy-de-Provence. The painting is known for its bold use of colors and thick brushstrokes, which create a sense of movement and depth. The painting is considered a masterpiece as it is an early representation of the artist's use of bold colors and thick brushstrokes.

The museum also features a section dedicated to the artist's drawings, which offer a glimpse into his creative process and the development of his style. Visitors can see how he experimented with different mediums and techniques, such as charcoal and pastels, to create his iconic works. This section of the museum is a must-see for art lovers and enthusiasts as it provides an in-depth look into the artist's creative process. Visitors can see how Van Gogh used different mediums and techniques to create his famous works and how he experimented with different styles and techniques.

Understanding The Artist's Life And Influences

The Van Gogh Museum provides a detailed and comprehensive look into the life and influences of the iconic artist, Vincent van Gogh. Visitors can learn about the artist's early years, his time in Paris and Arles, and his final days in Auvers-sur-Oise.

The museum covers Van Gogh's time in the Netherlands, where he grew up and began his artistic journey. Visitors can see examples of his early work, such as drawings and paintings of the Dutch countryside, which show the influence of the artists of the Hague School.

One of the most significant periods of Van Gogh's life was his time in Paris, where he was exposed to the new art movements of the day, such as Impressionism and Pointillism. Visitors can see how these influences shaped his work, with examples of paintings and drawings that show his experimentation with different styles and techniques.

The museum also covers Van Gogh's time in Arles, where he lived for a year and produced some of his most famous works, such as "The Starry Night." Visitors can learn about the artist's relationship with the town and how the vibrant colors and light of the south of France influenced his work.

Finally, the museum covers Van Gogh's final days in Auvers-sur-Oise, where he died at the age of 37. Visitors can learn about the artist's struggles with mental illness and how it affected his work during this period.

One of the most fascinating aspects of the museum is its focus on the artist's relationships and correspondences with other artists, including Paul Gauguin, Emile Bernard, and Paul Signac. Visitors can see letters and sketches exchanged between the artists, which offer a unique insight into the artistic community of the time and how Van Gogh was influenced by his peers.

In addition, the museum also covers the influence of Japanese art on Van Gogh's work, which can be seen in the artist's use of bold colors, simplified forms, and asymmetrical composition.

Special Exhibitions And Interactive Displays

The Van Gogh Museum is known for its rotating exhibitions that provide visitors with a deeper understanding of the artist's work and life. These special exhibitions focus on specific themes or periods of the artist's life, and are curated to provide new insights and perspectives on his art.

For example, in the past, the museum has featured exhibitions such as "Van Gogh and Japan," which explored the artist's love and fascination with Japanese art and culture, and how it influenced his work. Another exhibition, "Van Gogh and the Colors of the Night," examined the artist's use of color and light in his night paintings, and how they reflected his emotional state.

These exhibitions are not only a great way to see the artist's work in a new light, but also provide a deeper understanding of the cultural and historical context in which they were created.

In addition to the special exhibitions, the Van Gogh Museum also features interactive displays that allow visitors to explore the artist's work in a new and exciting way. For example, the museum has a virtual reality experience that takes visitors on a journey through some of the artist's most famous paintings, such as "The Starry Night." Visitors can explore the painting in a 360-degree view and see the details and brushstrokes up close.

The museum also features a digital art wall that displays a selection of the artist's works in high-resolution, allowing visitors to see the details and nuances of the paintings in a new way. The museum also has a special section for children where they can learn about Van Gogh's art and life through interactive activities and games.

Overall, the special exhibitions and interactive displays at the Van Gogh Museum offer a unique and engaging way to explore the artist's work and life, and are a must-see for any visitor.

CHAPTER 7: The Red Light District - A Walk Through Amsterdam's Most Infamous Neighborhood

Exploring The Red-Light District

The Red Light District, also known as De Wallen in Dutch, is one of the most famous neighborhoods in Amsterdam. It is located in the heart of the city, and is known for its vibrant nightlife, its many coffee shops, and its notorious red-light district. The area is full of narrow streets and canals, and is home to some of the most iconic buildings in the city.

As you walk through the streets of the Red Light District, you will be greeted by the colorful and lively atmosphere of the neighborhood. The streets are lined with shops and cafes, and there are plenty of opportunities to take in the local culture. You will also see many women standing in windows, dressed in lingerie, advertising their services as prostitutes. The red-light district is a unique place where the sex industry is legal, and you can see the women in the windows with red lights on, indicating they are available.

One of the main streets in the Red Light District is the Oudezijds Achterburgwal. This street is home to some of the oldest and most iconic buildings in the area, and is lined with shops, cafes, and restaurants. You will also see many of the famous red-light windows here, making it a popular spot for tourists.

Another popular spot in the Red Light District is the Oudezijds Voorburgwal. This street is home to many of the famous coffee shops in the area, and is known for its relaxed and laid-back atmosphere. Many visitors come here to take in the local culture and to sample some of the famous Dutch marijuana.

The Red Light District is also home to many museums and art galleries, such as the Museum of Prostitution and the Museum of Erotic Art. These museums offer a unique and fascinating insight into the history and culture of the area, and are well worth visiting. You can also take a boat tour through the canals of the Red Light District, which is a great way to see the area from a different perspective.

Discovering The Cultural Significance Of The Area

The Red Light District has a rich history and cultural significance in Amsterdam. The area was first developed in the late 14th century, and was originally home to many sailors and traders. It quickly became a hub of activity, with many shops and businesses opening up in the area.

One of the most iconic buildings in the Red Light District is the Old Church, also known as the Oude Kerk. This beautiful medieval church is one of the oldest buildings in Amsterdam, and is a popular tourist destination. The church has a fascinating history, and is known for its stunning architecture and intricate carvings. Visitors can also climb the church tower for a panoramic view of the neighborhood.

Another cultural highlight in the Red Light District is the Museum of Prostitution. This unique museum provides visitors with an in-depth look into the history of prostitution in Amsterdam. It features exhibits on the lives of the women who worked in the area, as well as the cultural and political context of the time. The museum also offers guided tours, which provide an even more in-depth look into the history of the Red Light District.

In addition to museums and historical buildings, the Red Light District is also home to many art galleries. The Red Light District Art Gallery is a popular destination for art lovers, as it features works by local and international artists. The gallery showcases a wide range of styles, including contemporary and modern art.

Lastly, the Red Light District is also home to many street performers and musicians. Visitors can enjoy live music and performances while wandering the streets, adding to the lively atmosphere of the neighborhood.

Understanding The Current Laws And Regulations

The laws and regulations surrounding the Red Light District in Amsterdam have evolved over time to ensure the safety and well-being of both the women working in the area and the tourists visiting it.

Prostitution is legal in the Netherlands, but it is regulated by the government. Prostitutes in the Red Light District must be at least 21 years old, and must be registered with the city. They are also required to undergo regular health checkups and carry a health card to prove that they are free of sexually transmitted infections.

The city of Amsterdam also has strict rules in place to protect the rights of the women working in the Red Light District. They are required to have a safe and clean working environment, and are protected by laws against discrimination and exploitation. This includes laws that prohibit clients from asking for specific services or engaging in certain sexual acts, as well as laws that prohibit the use of drugs or physical force by clients.

In addition, the city also has strict regulations in place to control the number of tourists visiting the Red Light District. Visitors are not allowed to take photos of the women working in the windows, and the city has implemented a "no-staring" policy to protect the privacy and dignity of the women. This policy also aims to prevent harassment of women by tourists.

Furthermore, the city has also put in place measures to limit the number of sex workers in the Red Light District, as well as the number of windows used for prostitution. This is done to prevent the over-commercialization of the area and to maintain the balance of the neighborhood.

CHAPTER 8: The Flower Market - A Visit To Amsterdam's Iconic Flower Market

Exploring The Flower Market

Amsterdam's iconic flower market, or Bloemenmarkt, is a must-visit destination for any traveler with an interest in flowers and horticulture. Located on the banks of the city's picturesque canals, this floating market is the only one of its kind in the world and has been in operation since 1862.

The market is made up of a series of colorful houseboats, each one overflowing with a vast array of flowers, plants, and bulbs. From the vibrant tulips and daffodils that are synonymous with the Netherlands, to exotic orchids and succulents, the market has something to offer everyone.

One of the most striking things about the market is the sheer scale of it. There are over 15 houseboats to explore, each one brimming with a vast array of different flowers and plants. It is an ideal place to pick up a bouquet of flowers, a potted plant, or even a small tree.

In addition to the houseboats, there are also several permanent flower stalls lining the market, selling all manner of floral-related items, from vases and pots to gardening tools and books. It is a perfect place for flower enthusiasts as well as photographers who are looking for unique and colorful shots.

The market is open all days of the week and the best time to visit is in the morning when the flowers are fresh and the vendors are well-rested. The flower market is located in the heart of the city making it easy to access by foot, bike, or public transportation.

The market is not only a place to buy flowers, it's also an attraction in itself. The vendors are friendly and knowledgeable, and they are always happy to chat with visitors and offer advice on how to care for the flowers. The market also offers a great opportunity to learn about the different varieties of flowers and plants, as well as their cultural significance.

Finding The Best Tulip Bulbs

Tulips are one of the most popular flowers in the world, and there is no better place to find them than at Amsterdam's flower market, also known as the Bloemenmarkt. The market is renowned for its high-quality tulip bulbs, which are grown in the Netherlands' famous bulb fields. The Netherlands is known as the world's leading producer of tulip bulbs, and Amsterdam's flower market is the perfect place to find the best tulip bulbs.

When visiting the market, it is important to know that tulip bulbs are typically sold from September to May. During this time, you can find a wide variety of tulip bulbs to choose from, including the classic Dutch tulip, the frilly parrot tulip, and the delicate lily tulip. Each variety has its own unique characteristics, such as color, shape, and size, so it's worth taking some time to explore the different options available.

When looking for the best tulip bulbs, it's important to choose bulbs that are firm and heavy for their size. This is a sign that the bulbs are healthy and will grow well. It's also a good idea to examine the bulbs for any signs of mold or rot, as these can indicate that the bulbs are not of good quality. Additionally, it's a good idea to ask the vendor for their advice on when to plant the bulbs, as well as the best way to care for them. They would be the best person to give you tips and advice based on the local climate and soil conditions.

One of the best things about buying tulip bulbs at the flower market is that you can see the tulips in full bloom, which can help you decide which variety you want to plant in your garden. Additionally, many vendors also sell pre-packaged tulip bulb collections which can be a great way to try out different varieties, without having to commit to buying large quantities of one specific type.

Discovering The Art Of Dutch Flower Arranging

Dutch flower arranging, also known as "Boerenbont," is a traditional style of flower arranging that is characterized by its use of wildflowers and natural materials. This style of flower arranging is deeply rooted in Dutch culture and history and is still very popular in the Netherlands today.

The flower market is the perfect place to learn more about this unique style of flower arranging. Many of the vendors are experts in the art of Boerenbont and are more than happy to share their knowledge and expertise with visitors.

One of the key elements of Dutch flower arranging is the use of wildflowers and natural materials, such as twigs, branches, and leaves. These elements are used to create a sense of natural beauty and simplicity that is both elegant and understated. The bouquet or arrangements are usually arranged in a way that the flowers appear to be growing naturally, rather than being forced into a particular shape.

Another important aspect of Boerenbont is the use of contrasting colors and textures. The arrangements often include a mix of different types of flowers, such as large and small flowers, spiky and delicate flowers, and flowers in different shades of the same color. This creates a sense of depth and movement in the arrangement that is both striking and eye-catching.

If you're interested in learning more about Dutch flower arranging, be sure to take a look at the beautiful bouquets and arrangements on display at the market. Many vendors offer workshops and classes in Boerenbont, where you can learn the techniques and principles of this traditional style of flower arranging. And if you're feeling inspired, you can even purchase your own flowers and materials and try your hand at creating your own Boerenbont arrangement.

CHAPTER 9: The Jordaan - A Tour Of The Charming And Historic Neighborhood

Exploring The Jordaan's History

The Jordaan is a charming and historic neighborhood located in the heart of Amsterdam, known for its picturesque canals, winding streets, and charming 17th and 18th-century houses. The neighborhood has a rich history that dates back to the 17th century when it was first established as a working-class area for the city's artisans and merchants.

The Jordaan was named after the River Jordan, which was said to be a symbol of the area's humble beginnings. The neighborhood was once home to many of Amsterdam's poorest residents, who lived in cramped and overcrowded conditions. However, over time, the Jordaan has transformed into a trendy and upscale neighborhood, known for its bohemian atmosphere and vibrant culture.

One of the most iconic features of the Jordaan is its network of canals, which were built in the 17th century as part of the city's expansion plans. These canals were used for transportation and as a source of drinking water for the residents of the Jordaan. Today, they are a popular tourist attraction and a great place to explore on a canal boat tour.

Another important aspect of the Jordaan's history is its association with the Dutch Golden Age. The neighborhood was home to many of Amsterdam's most famous artists, including Rembrandt van Rijn, who lived and worked in the Jordaan in the 17th century. Today, visitors can see the house where Rembrandt lived, which has been converted into a museum dedicated to his life and work.

The Jordaan is also known for its historical monuments, including the Westerkerk, which is the largest church in Amsterdam and is famous for its bell tower, which offers stunning views of the city. The church is also the final resting place of many famous Dutch figures, including Rembrandt and his wife, Saskia.

Finding The Best Street Art

The Jordaan is a neighborhood that is well-known for its street art, with a wide range of colorful murals, graffiti, and street art to be found throughout the area. Street art in the Jordaan is a reflection of the neighborhood's bohemian and creative spirit, and is a great way to discover the area's unique character.

One of the best places to see street art in the Jordaan is on the Haarlemmerstraat, which is known for its diverse collection of murals and graffiti. This street is home to a number of street art galleries and studios, and is a great place to explore the neighborhood's street art scene. Visitors can expect to see a variety of styles and themes, from abstract and political to pop art and street art.

Another popular spot for street art in the Jordaan is the Brouwersgracht, which is home to a number of street art galleries and studios. Visitors can stroll along the canal and discover an array of colorful murals, graffiti, and street art. This is a great place to explore the neighborhood's street art scene, and visitors can expect to see a wide variety of styles and themes.

Another popular street art spot in the Jordaan is the "I Amsterdam" mural, located on the corner of the Haarlemmerstraat and the Prinsengracht. This iconic mural was created by street artist Eduardo Sanson and is a popular spot for visitors to take photos. The mural is a colorful and vibrant piece of street art that captures the spirit of the Jordaan and Amsterdam as a whole.

One of the most famous street art pieces in the Jordaan is the "Amsterdam Street Art" mural, located on the corner of the Haarlemmerstraat and the Prinsengracht. This mural was created by street artist Eduardo Sanson and is a popular spot for visitors to take photos. The mural is a colorful and vibrant piece of street art that captures the spirit of the Jordaan and Amsterdam as a whole.

In addition to the above-mentioned spots, the Jordaan is home to many other street art, and visitors can explore the neighborhood's winding streets and discover an array of colorful murals, graffiti, and street art. With so much to see and explore, street art in the Jordaan is a great way to discover the area's unique character and learn more about its vibrant culture and history.

Discovering The Hidden Gems Of Jordaan

The Jordaan is full of hidden gems that are waiting to be discovered by visitors. One of the most charming places to explore in the neighborhood is the Nine Streets, a collection of nine narrow streets that are lined with independent boutiques, vintage shops, and coffee shops.

Another hidden gem in the Jordaan is the Noordermarkt, a picturesque square that is home to a weekly farmer's market and a number of charming cafes and restaurants. The market is a great place to sample local cheeses, breads, and other traditional Dutch foods.

Another must-see hidden gem in the Jordaan is the Begijnhof, a secluded courtyard that is surrounded by historic houses and is home to the oldest house in Amsterdam. The Begijnhof is a peaceful and tranquil spot that is a great place to escape the hustle and bustle of the city.

The Jordaan is also home to a number of hidden gems that are dedicated to Amsterdam's rich cultural heritage. One of these is the Museum Willet-Holthuysen, a 17th-century canal house that has been converted into a museum dedicated to the lives of Amsterdam's wealthy merchants. The museum is filled with beautiful antiques and artwork, and offers a glimpse into Amsterdam's past.

Another hidden gem in the Jordaan is the Museum Van Loon, a 17th-century canal house that has been converted into a museum dedicated to the lives of Amsterdam's wealthy merchants. The museum is filled with beautiful antiques and artwork, and offers a glimpse into Amsterdam's past.

Finally, the Jordaan is home to a number of hidden gems that are dedicated to Amsterdam's rich cultural heritage. One of these is the Museum Het Schip, a museum dedicated to

Amsterdam's famous School of Amsterdam style of architecture. The museum is filled with beautiful antiques and artwork, and offers a glimpse into Amsterdam's past.

Conclusion And Additional Recommendations For Exploring Amsterdam

Amsterdam is a city that is rich in culture, history, and beauty. Known for its picturesque canals, charming architecture, and vibrant nightlife, Amsterdam is a destination that should not be missed. After spending several days exploring the city, it is easy to see why Amsterdam is one of the most popular tourist destinations in Europe.

Conclusion And Final Thoughts

Amsterdam is a city that is full of surprises. From the moment you step off the train, you are immediately struck by the charm and beauty of the city. The canals are a highlight of any visit to Amsterdam, and there are plenty of opportunities to take a boat tour or rent a bicycle to explore the city. The architecture in Amsterdam is also something that should not be missed. The city is home to some of the most beautiful buildings in Europe, including the

Rijksmuseum, the Anne Frank House, and the Van Gogh Museum.

The nightlife in Amsterdam is also something that should not be missed. Whether you are looking for a night out on the town, or a quiet evening in a cozy café, Amsterdam has something to offer. The city is home to a wide variety of bars, clubs, and restaurants, and there is always something happening.

Overall, Amsterdam is a city that is full of surprises. Whether you are interested in history, culture, or just a good time, Amsterdam has something to offer. It is a destination that should not be missed, and one that you will want to visit again and again.

Additional Recommendations For Activities And Events

There are plenty of activities and events to enjoy in Amsterdam, beyond the typical tourist attractions. One of the best ways to experience the city is by taking a bike tour.

Amsterdam is a very bike-friendly city, and there are plenty of bike rental shops to choose from. This is a great way to see the city at your own pace, and to explore some of the quieter, more residential areas.

Another great activity to try in Amsterdam is a cooking class. The Dutch cuisine is not as well-known as some of the other European cuisines, but it is definitely worth trying. A cooking class will give you the opportunity to learn about the local ingredients and how to prepare traditional dishes.

If you are interested in art and culture, the Stedelijk Museum is a must-see. This museum is home to one of the largest collections of modern and contemporary art in the world, and it is definitely worth a visit.

Finally, if you are looking for a unique experience, consider visiting the EYE Filmmuseum. This museum is dedicated to the art of film and it is a great way to learn about the history of Dutch film.

How To Make The Most Of Your Amsterdam Trip

To make the most of your Amsterdam trip, it is important to plan ahead. This means researching the different activities and events that are available, and making sure that you have enough time to see and do everything that you want to.

Another important thing to keep in mind is to be open to new experiences. Amsterdam is a city that is full of surprises, and there are always new things to discover. Be open to trying new things, and be willing to explore the city in new ways.

Finally, make sure to take advantage of the city's bike-friendly culture. Amsterdam is a great city to explore by bike, and it is a great way to see the city from a different perspective.

Amsterdam is a city that is full of surprises. Whether you are interested in history, culture, or just a good time, Amsterdam has something to offer. With so many activities and events to choose from, it is important to plan ahead and be open to new experiences. By following these recommendations and making the most of your trip, you will be able to fully immerse yourself in the city and create unforgettable memories.

Additionally, make sure to budget your time and money wisely. Amsterdam can be quite expensive, so it's important to plan accordingly and prioritize what you want to see and do. Try to book your accommodation and activities in advance, as this can help save money and ensure that you get to do everything you want to.

Lastly, make sure to take the time to relax and enjoy the city. Amsterdam is a very laid-back and relaxed place, and it's important to take a step back and take in all the beauty around you. Whether it's sitting by a canal, enjoying a beer at a local café, or just taking a leisurely stroll through the streets, make sure to take the time to fully experience Amsterdam.

In conclusion, Amsterdam is a city that should not be missed. With its charming canals, beautiful architecture, and vibrant nightlife, it is a destination that has something to offer everyone. By following these recommendations and making the most of your trip, you will be able to fully immerse yourself in the city and create unforgettable memories.

BONUS CHAPTER: 14-Days Trip Plan To Amsterdam

Day 1

- Arrive in Amsterdam and check into your hotel.
- Take a leisurely stroll along the canals, exploring the winding streets and taking in the beautiful architecture.
- Have dinner at a traditional Dutch restaurant, such as a "brown café" or a "stroopwafel" stand.

Day 2

- Start the day at the Rijksmuseum, where you can explore the vast collection of Dutch art and history.
- In the afternoon, take a guided tour of the Anne Frank House to learn about the history of the Frank family and their time in hiding during World War II.

- In the evening, enjoy a canal cruise to see Amsterdam from a different perspective.

Day 3

- Visit the Heineken Experience, where you can learn about the brewing process and taste different varieties of Heineken.
- In the afternoon, head to the Van Gogh Museum to see some of the artist's most famous works.
- In the evening, have dinner at a trendy restaurant in the Jordaan neighborhood, known for its charming streets and local boutiques.

Day 4

- Take a guided tour of the Red Light District to learn about the history and culture of this famous area.
- In the afternoon, visit the Flower Market, where you can find a wide variety of flowers and plants.

- In the evening, take a bike ride around the city to see the beautiful architecture and canals at night.

Day 5

- Visit the Amsterdam Museum to learn more about the city's history and culture.
- In the afternoon, take a trip to the nearby town of Haarlem, known for its picturesque streets and lively market square.
- In the evening, enjoy dinner at a traditional Dutch restaurant, such as a "brown café" or a "stroopwafel" stand.

Day 6

- Start the day at the Dutch National Opera and Ballet, where you can see a performance or take a tour of the theater.

- In the afternoon, visit the Vondelpark, Amsterdam's largest park, where you can relax, have a picnic, or take a bike ride.
- In the evening, head to the Leidseplein, a lively square known for its bars, restaurants, and nightlife.

Day 7

- Visit the Stedelijk Museum, which specializes in contemporary art and design.
- In the afternoon, take a trip to the nearby town of Zaanse Schans, known for its traditional Dutch windmills and clog-making workshops.
- In the evening, enjoy dinner at a trendy restaurant in the Jordaan neighborhood, known for its charming streets and local boutiques.

Day 8

- Start the day at the Dutch National Museum of Ethnology, which explores the cultures of the world.

- In the afternoon, visit the NEMO Science Museum, where you can learn about science and technology through interactive exhibits.
- In the evening, head to the Leidseplein, a lively square known for its bars, restaurants, and nightlife.

Day 9

- Visit the Hermitage Amsterdam, which hosts temporary exhibitions from the State Hermitage Museum in St. Petersburg.
- In the afternoon, take a trip to the nearby town of Edam, known for its cheese-making workshops and charming streets.
- In the evening, enjoy dinner at a traditional Dutch restaurant, such as a "brown café" or a "stroopwaf"

Day 10

- Spend the day at the Amsterdam Zoo, where you can see a wide variety of animals from around the world.

- In the afternoon, take a guided tour of the Royal Palace of Amsterdam, the official residence of the Dutch royal family.
- In the evening, head to the trendy De Pijp neighborhood, known for its international food scene and cozy bars.

Day 11

- Visit the Jewish Historical Museum, which explores the history and culture of Amsterdam's Jewish community.
- In the afternoon, take a trip to the nearby town of Delft, known for its picturesque streets, canals, and famous Delftware pottery.
- In the evening, enjoy dinner at a trendy restaurant in the Jordaan neighborhood, known for its charming streets and local boutiques.

Day 12

- Start the day at the Tropenmuseum, which explores the cultures of the world, with a special focus on non-Western cultures.
- In the afternoon, take a guided tour of the Artis Royal Zoo, which is home to a wide variety of animals and plants.
- In the evening, head to the Leidseplein, a lively square known for its bars, restaurants, and nightlife.

Day 13

- Visit the Museum Het Schip, which explores the history and architecture of Amsterdam's famous "Ship" housing complex.
- In the afternoon, take a trip to the nearby town of Leiden, known for its picturesque streets, canals, and historic university.
- In the evening, enjoy dinner at a traditional Dutch restaurant, such as a "brown café" or a "stroopwafel" stand.

Day 14

- Spend your last day in Amsterdam exploring the city on your own, visiting any sights or neighborhoods that you may have missed.
- In the evening, pack your bags and prepare for your journey home.

Note: The above itinerary is just a suggestion and can be modified as per your convenience and preference, you can also add any other place you wish to visit.

Made in the USA
Middletown, DE
28 February 2023

25870618R00049